16

W9-BML-271

\

St. Patrick's Day

Parades, Shamrocks, and Leprechauns

Elaine Landau

Enslow Publishers, Inc.

40 Industrial Road   PO Box 38
Box 398   Aldershot
Berkeley Heights, NJ 07922   Hants GU12 6BP
USA   UK

http://www.enslow.com

For Jason Garmizo

Library of Congress Cataloging-in-Publication Data

Landau, Elaine.
  St. Patrick's Day / Elaine Landau.
    p. cm. — (Finding out about holidays)
  Includes bibliographical references and index.
  ISBN 0-7660-1777-X
  1. Saint Patrick's Day—Juvenile literature. I. Title: Saint
Patrick's Day. II. Title. III. Series.
GT4995.P3 L36 2002
394.262—dc21

                              2001005560

Printed in the United States of America

10 9 8 7 6 5 4 3 2 1

To Our Readers: We have done our best to make sure all Internet addresses in the book were active and appropriate when we went to press. However, the author and the publisher have no control over and assume no liability for the material available on those Internet sites or on other Web sites they may link to. Any comments or suggestions can be sent by e-mail to comments@enslow.com or to the address on the back cover.

Photo Credits: Associated Press, p. 38; Cheryl Wells, p. 43 (all); © Corel Corporation, pp. 4, 6, 8, 9, 11, 12, 14 (top), 18, 19 (background), 20, 21, 22, 24, 27, 36, 40 (both), 41, 42-43 (background), 44, 45, 46, 48; Dover Publications, Inc., p. 13; Enslow Publishers, Inc., pp. 10, 14 (left), 29, 35, 39; Harry Kerr/Hulton Getty/Archive Photos, p. 19 (ineset); Hemera Technologies, Inc., pp. i, ii, iii, 5, 7 (both), 15, 23, 26 (bottom), 33 (both); Images © 1995 Photo Disc, Inc., p. 16; Joseph Faria, pp. 25, 26 (top); Mary O'Connor, pp. 34 (both), 47; Photograph courtesy of www.sacredsites.com and Martin Gray, p. 17; REUTERS/Ferran Paredes/Archive Photos, pp. 31, 32; REUTERS/Mark Caldwell/Archive Photos, p. 28; REUTERS/Mike Brown/Archive Photos, p. 37; REUTERS/Peter Morgan/Archive Photos, p. 30.

Cover Photo: Enslow Publishers, Inc. (background), REUTERS/Mark Caldwell/Archive Photos (top inset), Hemera Technologies, Inc. (middle inset), Joseph Faria (bottom inset).

CONTENTS

1 The Greenest Day 5

2 At the Start 9

3 A Special Calling 17

4 Legends and Symbols 23

5 Let's Celebrate 29

   St. Patrick's Day Craft Project 42

   Words to Know 44

   Reading About 46

   Internet Addresses 47

   Index 48

St. Patrick's Day is an important holiday in Ireland.

CHAPTER 1

The Greenest Day

March 17 is a special day. Many people wear green that day. Classrooms and businesses are decorated in green. School cafeterias serve green Jell-O. Bakeries sell green cupcakes. In Chicago, Illinois, green dye is put into the Chicago River to turn the water green for a day. March 17 is Saint Patrick's Day. It is an Irish holiday and a day for everyone to wear the color green.

Ireland is a country in Europe. It has miles of green fields and valleys. Ireland even has a special name. It is known as the Emerald Isle.

IRELAND'S FLAG

The national flag of Ireland is called the "Tricolor." The orange part stands for one of the major religious groups of Ireland, the Protestants. The green part stands for the other major religious group, the Irish Catholics. And the white part stands for peace between the people of both religions.

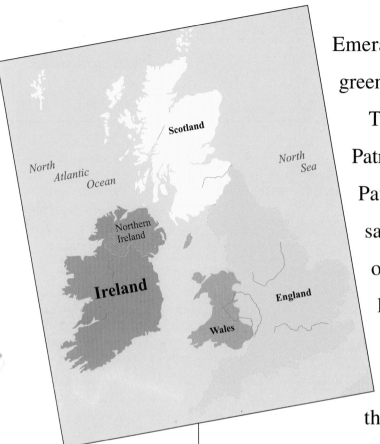

Ireland is an island in the North Atlantic Ocean.

Emeralds are beautiful bright green jewels.

The Irish celebrate St. Patrick's Day every year. St. Patrick is Ireland's patron saint. A patron saint watches over people and places and keeps them safe. The Irish people believe not only that St. Patrick protects them, but also that he brought the Christian religion to Ireland.

St. Patrick's Day is celebrated outside of Ireland, too. There are St. Patrick's Day celebrations wherever Irish people live, including in the United States.

In many ways, St. Patrick's Day has become an American holiday. It is not celebrated throughout the country. It is not an official government holiday like Presidents' Day. Schools, banks, and businesses are all open on St. Patrick's Day. The mail is delivered, too. But everyone is welcome to celebrate St. Patrick's Day. Even people who are not Irish can enjoy the day. March 17 is a day for parades, parties, and having fun. So on St. Patrick's Day, put on something green and join the fun!

Emeralds are precious gems. They are usually a deep green color.

St. Patrick's Cathedral
in Dublin, Ireland.

CHAPTER 2

At the Start

ST. PATRICK'S CATHEDRAL

Dublin, Ireland, is home to one of the largest—and most famous—churches in Ireland. St. Patrick's Cathedral was built in 1191, and in 1320, it became Ireland's first university. Many people visit the cathedral every year to pray and to learn about the history of this special church.

St. Patrick's Day is an Irish holiday, but St. Patrick was not Irish. His name was not even Patrick.

St. Patrick was born somewhere in the British Isles, the area that includes England, Scotland, and Wales. Yet St. Patrick was not British, either. He was probably born in the year 385. At that time, people from Rome, Italy, ruled the land. So Patrick grew up as a Roman.

Not much is known about Patrick's childhood. But we think that his name was Maewyn Succat. Patrick's father was an important worker in the Roman government.

St. Patrick is one of the most famous people in Irish history, but he was not born in Ireland.

Their family had a lot of money and lived in a large house by the sea. Servants waited on them.

As a boy, Patrick did not seem very saintly. He did not pray all the time. He did not always listen to the priests. However, that all changed when trouble started in Ireland, which was called Hibernia then.

Fierce fighting tribes lived in Hibernia, across the sea from the British Isles. The men of these tribes often raided other lands. They stole things, took people hostage, and returned to Hibernia, where the people were sold as slaves.

When he was just sixteen, Patrick was kidnapped by raiders from Hibernia. Some of his family's servants were taken, too. A powerful chief named Miliuc bought Patrick to Hibernia to be his slave.

Miliuc owned many sheep. Patrick became a shepherd. He watched over his master's sheep and lived outside with the animals. He made sure that the animals did not run away.

It was a hard life. There were many cold and rainy nights. Patrick felt very lonely and sad. He wondered why he had been captured. He thought that God might be punishing him. He wished that he had listened to the priests.

Patrick was a shepherd for six years. During that time, he became very religious. He prayed often and he began to have visions. He believed God was appearing before him and speaking to him.

One night, Patrick heard a special voice that brought some welcome news. The voice told

For six years, Patrick looked after his master's sheep.

Patrick believed that God appeared to him in visions.

Patrick he would go home soon. It told him that a ship was ready to take him home.

Patrick was far away from the sea. It was dangerous for him to try to go there. A slave who ran away could be killed. But Patrick believed that God wanted him to go.

Patrick traveled over two hundred miles. Finally, he reached the sea where he found a ship waiting for him.

Patrick wanted to get on the ship. But, at first, the ship's captain would not help him. He saw that Patrick was a runaway slave. Helping a runaway slave was dangerous. If the captain got caught, he could be punished.

Patrick left, but he did not know what to do next. So, he began to pray.

Perhaps Patrick's prayers were heard. Suddenly people on the ship called out to him.

They told Patrick to come back. The captain had changed his mind.

Patrick wanted to go home. But that did not happen. There were storms at sea, and the ship crashed.

The men ended up in a place that seemed to be deserted. There was no food in sight. It looked like they might die from hunger. Nearly a month passed, and the men grew very weak.

Patrick's ship was wrecked because of wild storms at sea.

13

When they spotted a herd of wild pigs, the captain believed that God had answered Patrick's prayers.

This figure is a Celtic sculpture of a wild pig.

Patrick asked God to save them. He also prayed for food. Before long, the men spotted a herd of wild pigs. No one knew where the pigs came from. But the captain thought that Patrick's prayers had been answered.

The men caught some of the pigs. They would now have food—and with food, they would not starve.

No one really knows what happened after

14

that. Patrick later wrote that he became a slave again. No one knows for sure who captured him. Some people say a group of fighting men found the ship's crew and all the men except Patrick were sold as slaves. The story says that the group of fighting men kept Patrick with them.

But there is another story about the ship's captain. The captain believed in Patrick. He had seen him pray for food. The captain never wanted to be hungry again. So he forced Patrick to stay close.

We do not know which story is true. But Patrick was not a slave for very long. Once again, he heard a voice. This time, the voice said that Patrick would be free in two months. And he was!

Patrick did not want to be a slave again.

There is also a St. Patrick's Cathedral in New York City. It is a beautiful church that is found among the towering skyscrapers in Manhattan.

A Special Calling

Patrick was finally free and he knew what he wanted to do. When he was a slave, he had not been allowed to go to school. Now he wanted to study religion. Patrick went to France and learned all he could. He became a priest.

In the year 432, Patrick was made a bishop. This is an important position in the Catholic Church. The pope is the head of the Catholic Church. He gave the new bishop the name Patricius, Latin for Patrick.

Patrick also returned to his homeland. He had been gone for many years. His family was very

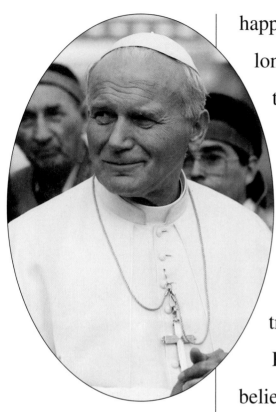

This is Pope John Paul II. He is the head of the Catholic Church.

happy to see him. But he did not stay home for long. Patrick believed that God wanted him to go back to Ireland.

Patrick wanted the Irish to love God. He hoped that they would become Christians. Patrick gathered together a group of priests. They set sail for Ireland. It would be the most important trip of Patrick's life.

People in Ireland had many different beliefs. They prayed to many gods. Magic was part of their religion, too.

Many different chiefs also ruled over Ireland. Each chief had his own religious advisers They were known as Druids.

The Druids prayed to different gods of nature. They held secret ceremonies in oak forests. Druids were thought to have strong magical powers. People believed that the Druids could see the future.

The Druids made life very difficult for Patrick. They thought he was their enemy. The Druids said that Patrick was evil. They even tried to kill him.

But Patrick would not leave Ireland. He wanted people to become Christians and

The Druids (inset) held ceremonies and prayed to many different gods of nature. Stonehenge (below) is a place where Druids once worshipped.

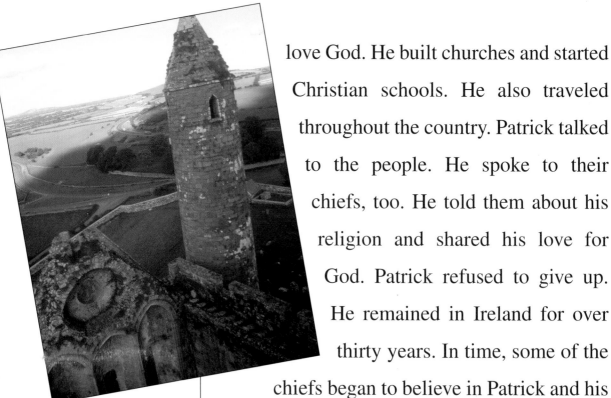

St. Patrick travelled the countryside to teach religion.

love God. He built churches and started Christian schools. He also traveled throughout the country. Patrick talked to the people. He spoke to their chiefs, too. He told them about his religion and shared his love for God. Patrick refused to give up. He remained in Ireland for over thirty years. In time, some of the chiefs began to believe in Patrick and his faith. The chiefs and their followers became Christians. They felt his kindness and they began to believe his words.

Patrick did what he had hoped to do. He helped thousands of Irish people find God. He helped turn Ireland into a Christian land.

Patrick died on March 17 in the year 461. After his death, the Church made him a saint.

A saint is someone who is officially recognized by the Church for holiness.

We celebrate St. Patrick's Day on the day of Patrick's death. In Ireland, it is a religious holiday. People honor St. Patrick by going to special church services. They also enjoy getting together with family and friends.

Special services are held at churches on St. Patrick's Day.

The Irish people are famous for special Celtic designs in their artwork. Some of the patterns look woven, like a basket. This is a cross with a Celtic design.

CHAPTER 4

Legends and Symbols

People believe that it is lucky to find a four-leaf clover. They also believe that the leaves have special meanings. The first leaf stands for faith. The second leaf stands for hope. The third leaf stands for love. The fourth leaf stands for luck.

Many stories about St. Patrick have been told through the years. These stories are known as legends.

One St. Patrick's Day legend is about snakes. It says that St. Patrick cast a spell over the snakes of Ireland. Some people say he beat a drum to frighten the snakes. Then the snakes crawled into the sea. Ireland was free from snakes forever.

Another St. Patrick's Day legend is about shamrocks. A shamrock is a small green plant with three leaves. It looks like a clover. St. Patrick used the three leaves of the shamrock to

It is believed that St. Patrick drove all the snakes in Ireland into the sea.

teach people in Ireland about the Holy Trinity. The shamrock's three leaves are part of the same plant. The Father, the Son, and the Holy Spirit are all part of one God. The shamrock became a symbol of St. Patrick and a symbol of Ireland.

Irish fairies and leprechauns are also symbols of St. Patrick's Day. Both were believed to be small magical spirits. The Druids had believed in magic. But St. Patrick's teaching made these things less important. In stories, the spirits became smaller in size, too. People spoke of the magic of the "little people" or "wee folk."

Irish fairies are supposed to love to dance. Stories say they twirled and whirled all day, and wore out their shoes. People believed that there were also little men who mended the fairies' shoes. They dressed in green, wore cocked hats and leather aprons, and carried tools for fixing shoes. They were leprechauns.

Leprechauns worked at night, repairing shoes while the fairies slept. The fairies left gold coins for the leprechauns to pay them for their work. The leprechauns carefully saved their coins. Stories say they had large pots filled with all of their gold coins.

Irish stories were often told with music. Sometimes people would play a harp, a stringed instrument that has a pleasing tone. The

Irish people believed that fairies were tiny, magical creatures who danced and played all day.

harp is one of Ireland's oldest instruments. It has also become a symbol of Ireland.

On St. Patrick's Day, we see many symbols. Harps are played. Children hear stories about leprechauns and Irish fairies.

When people wear green it is called the "wearing of the green." The color reminds us of the shamrock. On March 17, the spirit of Ireland comes alive. We know it is St. Patrick's Day.

Leprechauns are tiny imaginary men who are known for hiding pots of gold.

Harps are beautiful-sounding stringed instruments.

St. Patrick's Day is also a day for parades.

CHAPTER 5

Let's Celebrate

St. Patrick's Day is not a new holiday. It has been celebrated in the United States for a long time. In the 1700s, many people from Ireland came to America, hoping to start a better life. They had celebrated St. Patrick's Day in Ireland. They did the same in their new country, the United States.

The first official St. Patrick's Day celebration in the United States was in Boston, Massachusetts in 1737. Many Irish people settled there. They had a St. Patrick's Day parade.

St. Patrick's Day parades are still common

CLADDAGH RING

★

Claddagh rings date back hundreds of years. In the 1600s, they were often exhanged by friends or lovers. Each of the ring's three parts have special meanings. The heart stands for love. The hands stand for faith and friendship. The crown stands for loyalty.

today. Over 120 cities in the United States have them. The largest parade is in New York City. But Chicago, Illinois and Philadelphia, Pennsylvania also have big parades.

St. Patrick's Day parades are exciting. High school bands play, and sometimes there are clowns and horses. Children dressed as leprechauns and fairies may march in the parade.

Often people from Irish clubs are in the parade. Many people wear green costumes. They might pass out green flowers to the people watching.

Some people wear festive face paint on St. Patrick's Day.

31

Many people dress in green and wave Irish flags during St. Patrick's Day parades.

Everyone comes out to cheer and watch the people in the parade. They might wave small Irish flags or twirl long green ribbons. Children hold on to green balloons. Everyone claps when their favorite band passes.

In Manchester, New Hampshire, it is easy to figure out where the parade starts. A giant shamrock is painted on that spot. Marchers in the St. Patrick's Day parade in Milwaukee, Wisconsin, always enjoy the view. Businesses along the parade route decorate their windows. There is even a contest for the best-decorated window. Judges pick the winner before the parade begins.

Parades are great. But there are also other things to enjoy on St. Patrick's Day. Many schools celebrate the holiday. Children often make green decorations. They might hang up paper shamrocks and leprechaun hats. Sometimes there are St. Patrick's Day parties. Green cupcakes and cookies are always

It's fun to wear hats with shamrocks on them for St. Patrick's Day!

Irish dancers perform on St. Patrick's Day.

popular. Chocolate coins in gold foil are fun, too. These look like gold from a leprechaun's pot.

Some schools have special St. Patrick's Day activities. An Irish storyteller may be invited. Sometimes Irish dancers perform. St. Patrick's Day contests are fun, too. There may be a contest for the best St. Patrick's Day poster. A prize might also go to the boy or girl wearing the most green.

St. Patrick's Day festivals are also held all over the United States. There is always Irish music. You can see Irish dancers, too. Some are local dance groups. Others come from Ireland for the festival.

All sorts of Irish crafts may be put on

display. Sometimes people watch the crafts being made. Irish glassblowers make vases. Irish silversmiths work with silver to make rings and bracelets. Often the jewelry has Irish symbols on it.

Beauty contests are also part of many St. Patrick's Day festivals. The winner is named the festival queen. She will wear a

People like to wear jewelry with Celtic designs.

crown and sit on a special throne. Her title may be "Miss Shamrock" or "Miss Irish Rose."

The festivals always have special children's events. There are St. Patrick's Day puppet shows. Young people also learn old Irish songs. Often they can watch sheepdogs at

Sheepdogs keep the sheep safe in Ireland.

work. Sheepdogs are very important in Ireland. They keep the sheep together in the fields.

On St. Patrick's Day, the Chicago River is dyed green.

The Irish Fair in St. Paul, Minnesota is a very large event. It is a two-day celebration. Thousands of people attend. For them, it is a great way to enjoy St. Patrick's Day.

Each year, the Empire State Building is lit up with green lights in honor of St. Patrick's Day.

Other people choose athletic events to celebrate the holiday. They may sign up for St. Patrick's Day races. One St. Patrick's Day race is held in Colorado Springs, Colorado. Nearly five hundred runners take part. Afterward there is a one-mile race for children. All the young runners get prizes.

New York City has the country's biggest St. Patrick's Day parade. It also has one of the nation's biggest buildings—the Empire State Building. On St. Patrick's Day the Empire State Building is lit up in green. This famous skyscraper has a special tie to St. Patrick. Construction on it began on March 17, 1930. Many of the workers there were Irish. They were especially proud that they were working on this terrific building, and that the work was starting on St. Patrick's Day.

St. Patrick's Day can be fun anywhere. In many cities, water fountains spray green water. Irish clubs have St. Patrick's Day breakfasts. They even serve green pancakes.

Restaurants also have special St. Patrick's

Irish stew and corned beef and cabbage are two popular dishes served on St. Patrick's Day.

Day menus. They serve tasty Irish dishes like corned beef and cabbage and Irish stew.

Many families get together for the holiday. They may share a meal or sing Irish songs. St. Patrick's Day is a more religious holiday in Ireland than it is in the United States. But some people in the United States also go to church then. Churches often offer special St. Patrick's Day services.

On his holiday, Irish people remember St. Patrick and celebrate being Irish. But everyone can enjoy the festivities on St. Patrick's Day.

On St. Patrick's Day, many people enjoy desserts made with green food coloring.

St. Patrick's Day Craft Project

Leprechaun's Pot of Gold

You can have your own St. Patrick's Day treasure by making a pot of gold. You will need:

✔ **two-inch Dixie cup**

✔ **strip of black construction paper (2 inches wide and 6 inches long)**

✔ **20 pebbles or 10 stones**

✔ **gold magic marker or paint**

✔ **thin piece of green ribbon (8 inches long)**

✔ **white glue or tape**

1. Wrap the construction paper around the cup. Glue or tape the ends together. This is your pot for the gold.

2. Color each pebble with the gold magic marker or paint. These are your gold pieces.

3. Place the pebbles in the cup.

4. Tie a ribbon around the cup to add a touch of St. Patrick's Day green.

Safety Note: Be sure to ask for help from an adult, if needed, to complete this project.

St. Patrick's Day Craft Project

★

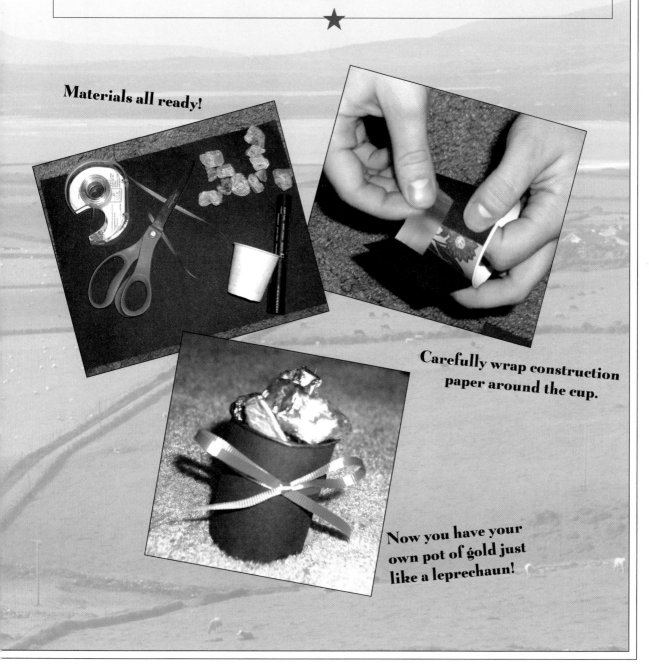

Materials all ready!

Carefully wrap construction paper around the cup.

Now you have your own pot of gold just like a leprechaun!

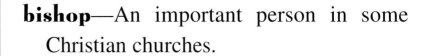

bishop—An important person in some Christian churches.

Druids—Religious advisers or priests in ancient Ireland.

emerald—A bright green precious jewel.

herd—A group of animals.

Hibernia—the name for ancient Ireland.

leprechaun—A small, magical, make-believe man. Stories said that leprechauns mended fairy shoes and had pots of gold.

Words to Know

★

patron saint—A saint who watches over and protects people and things.

shamrock—A small green plant with three leaves.

shepherd—A person who keeps the sheep together in the fields.

skyscraper—A very tall building.

symbol—Something that stands for something else.

vision—Something seen in a dream.

Reading About

Bevendes, Mary. *St. Patrick's Day Shamrocks*. Chanhassen, Minn.: Child's World, 1999.

Gibbons, Gail. *St. Patrick's Day*. New York: Holiday House, 1995.

January, Brendan. *Ireland*. Danbury, Conn.: Children's Press, 1999.

Ross, Kathy. *Crafts For St. Patrick's Day*. Brookfield, CT: Millbrook Press, 1999.

Internet Addresses

★

HISTORY AND CUSTOMS OF
ST. PATRICK'S DAY
<http://www.wilstar.com/holidays/patrick.htm>

ST. PATRICK'S DAY EVENTS AND HISTORY
<http://www.ireland.com/events/
    st.patricks/2001>

ST. PATRICK'S FUN AT KID'S DOMAIN
<http://www.kidsdomain.com/holiday/patrick/>

Index

★

B
Boston, Massachusetts, 29

C
Chicago, Illinois, 5, 30
Chicago River, 5
Colorado Springs, Colorado, 38
crafts, 34–35

D
Druids, 18, 19, 24

E
Empire State Building, 38

F
fairies, 24, 25, 26, 31
France, 17

G
green, 5, 6, 31, 32, 33, 38, 39

H
Hibernia, 10, 11

I
Ireland, 5, 6, 10, 18, 19, 20, 21, 23, 26, 29, 34, 37, 40

L
leprechauns, 24, 25, 26, 31, 33, 34

M
music, 25, 34

N
New York City, 30, 38

P
Philadelphia, Pennsylvania, 30

S
shamrock, 23, 24, 26, 33
sheepdogs, 36–37
snakes, 23
St. Patrick
    as a shepherd, 11
    birth, 9
    bishop in the Catholic Church, 17–20
    childhood, 10–11
    death, 20
    returns to Ireland, 18–20
St. Paul, Minnesota, 37